JUNIUS SMITH

Pioneer Promoter

of

Transatlantic Steam Navigation

By

E. LeRoy Pond

PUBLICATION OF

THE MARINE HISTORICAL ASSOCIATION, INC.

MYSTIC, CONNECTICUT

Vol. II. No. 2   March 31, 1941

PREFATORY NOTE

Not all credit for the modern ocean liner belongs to one man. It is the product of many minds. But to Junius Smith, Connecticut born citizen of the United States, belongs the unique distinction of promoting and putting in actual operation the first transatlantic steamship line; a service destined to affect most profoundly the future of the human race. That he accomplished his task in England and with the aid of British capital at a time when conservative financial and scientific opinion on both sides of the Atlantic regarded his project as visionary and impractical, lends added significance to his achievement, which thereby took rank as an impressive and, indeed, indispensable step in the development of Britain's modern sea power. It may be admitted that the ocean steamship would have come if the subject of this sketch had never been born. That is beyond doubt. It is equally beyond doubt that his vision, moral courage and tenacity of purpose advanced its coming by some—possibly by many—years. Nor should it seriously affect our appraisal of his service that, after a brief hour of dazzling fame, he met the all-too-common fate of great pioneers, dying in obscurity while the world profited by the experiment he set in motion. Samuel Cunard, in particular, and his able associates not only reaped the vast material rewards which Smith's revolutionary achievement had brought within reach, but, as so often happens, they also received from a forgetful public, undeserved and doubtless unwanted credit for the actual pioneer work he had completed. The account which follows presents briefly and, it is believed, with due consideration for the contributions of others, the facts which may serve to determine his rightful place in maritime history.

JUNIUS SMITH
Reproduced from an oil painting done in London in
1848, and formerly in the possession of his niece,
the late Mrs. William Lay, Chicago

Junius Smith

By E. LeRoy Pond

Junius Smith went to London originally on an errand involving a case in Admiralty Law. His brother David, of Smith, Woodward & Company of New Haven, Connecticut, British importers, had a ship *Mohawk* which had been seized and condemned as a prize by the British, and young Junius was dispatched in the autumn of 1805 to the High Court of Admiralty to argue the appeal. He had graduated from Yale College in 1802, had attended the Litchfield Law School with John C. Calhoun and at the age of twenty-three delivered the Fourth of July oration for the Connecticut Society of the Cincinnati.[1]

The parish of Northbury, now the town of Plymouth, Connecticut, in which he was born, October 2, 1780, was then a frontier village, and New Haven had more lawyers than it needed, but London was rich in litigation. The British prize courts, since Napoleon renewed his war with Great Britain, were full of condemnation proceedings against neutral vessels. At least 1,500 American ships were seized between 1803 and 1812;[2] they were sometimes taken at the rate of ten a week.[3] It is little wonder, then, that the young man remained in London, especially after the large damages which he won for his brother gave him an enviable prestige among American shippers.

Nor was it surprising that he soon became a shipper, himself. It was a remunerative occupation during the Napoleonic wars. His brother David moved from New Haven to New York, and they engaged in a transatlantic partnership. Junius visited Leeds, Birmingham, Sheffield and other manufacturing cities and shipped their products to David. David sent ships from the

---

(1)   Major David Smith, Junius's father, was a prominent member of this Society. The sword of one of two British officers whom he disarmed at Monmouth was presented to him by General Lafayette. The Connecticut Historical Society has his Valley Forge quarterbooks.
(2)   Day, Clive: "History of Commerce," 494
(3)   Medford, McCall: "Oil without Vinegar," 102.

West Indies, conforming to the British decree that neutral ships touch at a British port, and then Junius hurried them on to that port on the Continent that would yield the most profit. His own ships he registered under the neutral name of David and equipped them with French or British licenses as occasion might require to evade the blockades.[4] He could build his ships cheaper in America than his British competitors and owing to the war could obtain cheaper insurance at Lloyds.[5] A new power, steam, was doing the work of 3,000,000 men in England, and England not having the 3,000,000 men[6] who under the old community life would have consumed their own product, looked to the American shippers to carry away the surplus. England's exports to America constituted one-third of her exports to foreign countries.[7] They were three times what they were at the close of the American Revolution.[8]

Encouraged by this burst of prosperity, Junius decided to have a home of his own. He had met Sarah Allen, second daughter of Thomas Allen of Huddersfield, while on his trips to the manufacturing districts, and April 9, 1812, they were married. Then came the panic. The United States declared war, thus throwing away the neutrality upon which her shipping thrived, and Junius was ruined. In 1814 a daughter, Lucinda, was born. The family went to Liverpool for awhile but returned to London. It was not until the 30's, the days of his steamship activity, that we find them again enjoying prosperity.

The picture of Junius Smith in the 30's is that of a man five feet, five or six inches tall, with large head and noble countenance, drinking his tea and a little old port, a communicant of the Church of England, passionately fond of his garden. After the death, in 1836, of his wife—a handsome woman, so beautiful, it is said, that when she accompanied her husband to New York in 1832, she kept her face veiled when out on the street, to avoid the attention which she attracted—he moved with his daughter, Lucinda, who was twenty-two, from the home at Peckham Grove

(4)   Levi, L.: "History of British Commerce," 109, says 356 British licenses were issued in 1810.
(5)   Stephen, J.: "War in Disguise," 75-76.
(6)   Medford, McCall: "Observations on European Courts."
(7)   Cunningham, W.: "English Industry & Commerce," 519.
(8)   Medford, McCall: "Observations on European Courts."

to Perry Hill, Sydenham, later the site of the Crystal Palace.[9] From this country villa he walked a distance of eight miles each day to his office at No. 4 Fen Court, Fenchurch Street, except on such days as he could steal off to work in his garden, "for the daily walk," he explained, "is not exercise enough for my fat belly and heavy head." His New York partner, Henry, son of David, doing business under the name of Wadsworth & Smith, No. 4 Jones Lane, near 103 Front Street, was a cautious dealer, sometimes slow to follow the more adventuresome counsels of his uncle.

Shipping in 1830 was much different from that of 1805. The hazardous trade in many seas was supplanted by a direct trade from London to New York, made possible by the growth of America, the increased supply of manufactured goods in England, and the absence of prohibitive decrees. The population of the United States, which in 1805 was 6,000,000, had grown to be 12,866,000. New York had increased in population from 75,000 to 213,000. She was the second city in the world in the tonnage of her ships. The completion of the Erie Canal in 1825 made her the port of entrance for the rapidly developing Middle West, and she received over one-half the imports of the United States. Nearly all of the woolens, linens, cutlery, cotton goods, earthenware, hardware, and brass and cotton manufactures shipped from England to America came through her harbor.

The task of the Smiths was to find cargoes in America with which to pay for the manufactured goods. Cotton, flour and turpentine were the staples and there was money in the unusual shipments, such as birdseye maple, apples, cranberries, or clover seed. Occasionally the London merchant visited the docks, to investigate a complaint that turpentine had been so carelessly placed as to ruin the cotton or that goods had been stolen by wharf thieves, but most of his business was in the little office in the midst of the financial district. Here he scanned the newspapers and kept in close touch with the market, writing to his nephew as soon as he made up his mind what he wanted, and having the letter ready for the next packet that sailed to New York.

---

(9) Dr. Alexander Jones describes a visit there, in the New York "Journal of Commerce," February 12, 1853.

Another task was to obtain suitable vessels. It was essential to Smith, in order to keep ahead of his competitors, that he have in his service, under his exclusive control if possible, the best ships on the Atlantic.

The American packets in the 30's were the finest merchant vessels the world had seen. Besides passengers, for whom they were luxuriously equipped, they carried hardware, fine goods, salt, etc., and commanded rates much in excess of the freighters. In 1836 twenty packets were in service between New York and Liverpool, a dozen between New York and London, and fifteen between New York and Havre. The average time from New York to Liverpool was twenty days; from Liverpool to New York, owing to the prevalence of western winds, thirty-four days.[10] A phenomenal trip of fifteen days was made occasionally. Such a trip was a godsend to a shipper. Thus Nat Prime of New York made a small fortune, simply because his packet reached New York one Christmas Eve under unusually favorable winds, bringing news of the rise of the price of cotton. While his competitors were enjoying their Christmas holiday, Prime's messenger hastened to New Orleans and cornered the cotton market three days ahead of the public news.[11]

Yet the swiftest packets were powerless in a calm. Voyages of fifty or sixty days were not uncommon. Writers, ladies especially, who expected to write glowing descriptions of the ocean voyage, grew weary of the monotony, and the inspiration failed to come. Paganini abandoned his project of coming to America because of the time consumed in the journey.[12] The ship *William Thompson* from Liverpool, by rounding the dangerous north coast of Ireland, avoided a south wind and made half the trip across the ocean in nine days, a remarkable record, only to lie becalmed off the Banks of Newfoundland for twenty-three days, and the voyage lasted five weeks. "Towards the end of the voyage," said Stuart, describing a lottery as to the number of days before entering port, "a calm, or contrary wind occasioned a depression in value of one ticket, and the corresponding elevation of another, to as great an extent as in other times and in other

---

(10)   McCullough, J. H.: "Dictionary of Commerce," 837.
(11)   Barret, Walter: "Old Merchants of New York," I, 27.
(12)   Niles "Register," 1832, Vol. 43, p. 95.

funds Lord Rodney's victory or the battle of Waterloo."[13] Other ships which left England at the same time as did the *William Thompson* were longer on the water than she.

Packet voyages, moreover, were dangerous and uncomfortable. The tonnage of packets ranged from 450 to 800 tons, the average in 1830 being 600, no greater than that of some modern tugboats. If a ship sprang a leak, the only power to man the pumps was that of the human arm. If a fire started, the best known defense was a bucket brigade. Icebergs were a source of terror. In later years after ocean steamships were a success, Mrs. Sigourney pointed out the superiority of the steamship over a sailing vessel among icebergs. "The engine of the *Great Western*," she wrote, "accommodated itself every moment, like a living and intelligent thing, to the commands of the captain. 'Half a stroke!' and its tumultuous action was controlled; 'A quarter of a stroke!' and its breath seemed suspended; 'Stand still!' and our huge bulk lay motionless upon the waters, till two or three of the icy squadron drifted by us; 'Let her go!' and with the velocity of lightning we darted by another detachment of our deadly foes. It was then that we were made sensible of the advantages of steam, to whose agency, at our embarkation, many of us had committed ourselves with extreme reluctance. Yet a vessel more under the dominion of the winds, and beleaguered as we were amid walls of ice, in a rough sea, must inevitably have been destroyed."[14]

Junius Smith appreciated the speed of the packets. "Dispatch is the life and delay the death of all business connected with shipping," he wrote to his nephew. "If you had loaded turpentine, agreeable to orders, and loaded your ships without knowing too much, it is impossible to have prevented the making of a clear profit of 5,000 pounds. It may not be too late to do something yet, but the high price which was fairly in our hands is gone."

Yet he saw the disadvantages of the calms. They prevented him from getting word quickly to his nephew, from getting the favorable market price which had prevailed in London, and from

---

(13)   Stuart, J.: "Three Years in North America."
(14)   "Pleasant Memories of Pleasant Lands."

receiving perishable goods, such as apples, in sound condition. It galled his soul to think that his fortune depended on a mere passing breeze.

The remedy seemed simple. Steamboats were plying upon the rivers and along the coasts, especially in America, amazing the country-folk with their fires that shot into the night. A person could leave and arrive at a definite time. A merchant could know beforehand just what afternoon he could expect a hogshead of rum or a cask of sugar. "Why not found a steam packet line, ensuring both speed and certainty?" Smith asked the question while on a fifty-four days voyage to America in the British ship *St. Leonard* in 1832. The attraction such a vision would have for a practical idealist like Junius Smith is obvious, nor were its results long in appearing, as will be seen from the following letter which gives the earliest known account of his first energetic steps toward the development of transatlantic steam navigation:

London, Feb. 9, 1833.

Mr. Jones, Director of the London and Edinburgh Steam Packet Company.

Dear Sir,—In conjunction with my friends in New York, I am desirous of forming a line of steam-packets to run between this port and New York. I apprehend that four in number will be sufficient, and fully equal to the twelve American sailing ships now running on the same line; and the cost of the four steam-packets, at £30,000 each, will be about the same as the aggregate cost of the twelve American line of packets now running.

It is my intention to have two British and two American ships; and the reason is, first, to combine the interests of the two countries in their support; and secondly, to afford a certain conveyance both ways for goods of foreign as well as domestic growth and manufacture. By the treaty of commerce with the United States, British ships cannot take foreign goods into the United States, nor can American ships bring foreign goods from the United States to England for home consumption, but the converse is true of both. It will therefore be readily seen that a line formed of the ships of both nations, to sail alternately, will embrace all branches of the carrying trade. I left London for New York in August last, and the latter place for London on

700 TONS   320 H. P.

S. S. Sirius

From a print in the Stokes Collection published in 1838 showing arrival at New York, April 23rd, 1838

Reproduced by permission of the New York Public Library

the 20th December. My friends in New York make no doubt of the practicability nor of the success of such an undertaking, and have assured me that they will build two steam-vessels suited to the object in view, as soon as they learn that the plan, so far as regards the British interest, can be carried into execution here.

In New York, the plan is regarded as one of the first importance to the commercial interests of both countries.

I examined and travelled in many American steam-packets, but they have not one calculated for a sea voyage. They are all constructed to run upon the rivers, sounds, bays, and canals. These packets are in general very roomy, and calculated to carry many passengers.

The *North America*, in which I took passage on the 16th October, at New York, for Albany, 145 miles up the Hudson River, is 230 feet in length, 30 feet beam, has two 60-horse low-pressure engines, which work at the rate of 26 strokes of the piston per minute. This packet is calculated to accommodate 1,200 passengers, and there were 400 on board at the time mentioned. She draws but 4 feet of water, and performed the passage to Albany, against the current of the river, in twelve hours, including stoppages at the numerous landing-places on both sides of the river. Several other packets of nearly equal dimensions ply upon the river, a particular description of which is unnecessary here. The same general description of packets run in all the rivers, sounds, bays, etc., from which you will perceive their unfitness for the high seas.

The commercial intercourse between Great Britain and New York is of late years so amazingly increased, that more than 40,000 passengers and emigrants landed in the last year in the port of New York from Europe, chiefly from Great Britain.

Since the construction of the Erie Canal, running through the State of New York 350 miles, from Albany to Lake Erie, opening a water communication every step of the way from London to the Niagara Falls, the Lakes, Canada, Ohio, Michigan, and all the western part of the United States, now peopling with astonishing rapidity, and the establishment of elegant and convenient packet-boats upon the canal for the accommodation of passengers, New York has become the great thoroughfare for travellers and emigrants from every part of Europe. Whatever mode of conveyance will shorten and facilitate the passage from Europe, is certain to have a preference; and a line of steam-packets from London to New York would have not only the support of Great Britain, but of all Europe. I can hardly expect in a short letter to open up the subject so fully to those un-acquainted with the American trade, as to induce them to enter into my views fully at once, or to appreciate the commercial advantages which it promises. It was under this impression that I proposed, if the company entertained doubts as to the success of the undertaking, to charter of them a suitable vessel for two voyages, or two vessels for one voyage each, and to take upon myself the result of such an experiment.

The distance from Portsmouth to New York is about 3,000 miles, and a good packet ought to make the passage in twelve or thirteen days.

From March to October is generally the best season of the year for passengers, and if we sailed from London 20th April to 1st May, it would be in good time.

I am sure that no foreign port can offer such decided advantages for a line of steam-packets as New York, and up to the present time the ground is unoccupied.

I abstain at present from entering into any calculations as to the probable returns to New York. If these hints are not entertained, I should be glad to have them considered as confidential, and should feel obliged for as early an answer as practicable, for my future government.

Your obedient servant,

Junius Smith.

20, Abchurch-lane.

Little had been done in steamship navigation previous to 1832 except along the rivers and coasts of America and in Great Britain. The most notable long distance voyage was that of the steamer *Enterprise* in 1825 which went from London to Calcutta in 113 days, making numerous stops. A number of sailing vessels had crossed the Atlantic with steam auxiliary. The first of these was the American ship *Savannah*, 380 tons burden, whose advent off the coast of Ireland in 1819 created a sensation. Her paddle-wheels were constructed so as to fold up like a fan to be laid upon the deck when not in use.[15] Others were the *Conde de Patmella* which sailed in 1820 from Liverpool for Lisbon and went from there to the Brazils; the *Rising Star,* built in England for the navy of Chili and which arrived in Valparaiso in 1822, and the *Curacao,* 350 tons burden, with engines of 100 horsepower, which sailed from Antwerp to Curacao in the West Indies. These voyages accomplished little except to advertise the ships for the purpose of sale.

The second steamer to make the eastward crossing was the Canadian-built *Royal William,* which steamed from Pictou, in Nova Scotia, to Cowes, 2,500 miles, mostly if not entirely under steam.[16] This was in 1833.

"We were deeply laden with coal," wrote Captain McDougal, "deeper in fact than I would ever attempt covering the Atlantic with her again. However, we got on the Grand Bank of Newfoundland where we experienced a gale of wind which rather alarmed my engineer; he wished very much to go into Newfoundland. We had previously lost the head of our foremast, and one of the engines had become useless from the beginning of the gale; with the other we could do nothing, and the engineer reported the vessel to be sinking. Things looked rather awkward; however, we managed to get the vessel cleared of water, and ran by one engine after the gale ten days. After that we got along very well, and put into Cowes to clean the boilers, a job which generally occupied them from 24 hours to 26 every fourth day. However, we managed to paint her outside while there; the inside we had previously done, which enabled us to go up to London in fine style. Ten days after her arrival she was sold."[17]

The narrative of Captain McDougal is instructive as hinting at the problems that were to confront builders of Atlantic steamships. The crude engines were ravenous eaters. Thirteen steamers on the Hudson burned 1,600 cords of wood a week, the New York ferry boats burned 1,400 cords a week, and a

(15)   For Smith's comments on the claim of the "Savannah," see "Hunt's Merchants Magazine," February, 1847.
(16)   Sails were used as auxiliary by steamships long after steam became common on the Atlantic.
(17)   Letter to William King, Quebec, November 16, 1833, in "Transactions of Literary and Historical Society of Quebec," 1878.

Long Island steamer burned sixty cords each trip.[18] British ships used coal but it was of poor quality. Coal consumption per horsepower in 1834 was four times that of 1891.[19] Fuel took up so much space that there was no room for freight.[20] Ship architects proved that a transatlantic steamer would require coal bunkers larger than the vessel. Wooden ships could not be built longer than 300 feet owing to limits imposed by the strength of timber.

There were other difficulties besides that of fuel to discourage steam navigation upon the ocean. Devices for providing fresh water were not in use and steam vessels that ventured into salt water had to stop the engine every once in a while, not only to clean out the clinkers or to tighten the screws on the engine, but to blow the salt incrustations out of the boiler. Paddles, which gave good service on the rivers, were battered and mercilessly tossed by ocean waves. The pressure of steam was so low, that it is recorded of one of the early Atlantic steamers that she stopped to wind canvas and rope-yarn about a leaky steam-pipe, and then proceeded with the pipe thus under low pressure, meaning probably four or five pounds per square inch.[21]

An attempt was made in 1825 to found a steam line to New York from Valentia, on the west coast of Ireland. The idea was to have a number of steam vessels of 600 tons each, and an Act of Parliament was obtained for the formation of the Valentia Company. The terms of the Act were not complied with. In 1836, another company, the Dublin, proposing to avail itself of the favoring clauses in the Valentia Act, advertised for four pairs of the largest engines, and laid down a keel in Liverpool, but got no further. In the same year the British government dabbled in the Valentia scheme, by appointing a commission to inquire into such a project, as a sea-borne continuation of a proposed railway from Dublin to the West Coast.[22]

Dr. Dionysius Lardner, author of The Steam Engine and a prominent writer of his day, endorsed the Valentia project.

(18)   McMaster, V, 130.
(19)   Chadwick, F. E.: "Ocean Steamships," 9.
(20)   As an instance of improvement made in meeting the fuel problem in recent years, it is interesting to note that as late as 1864 a steamer of 3,000 tons had to give up 2,200 tonnage to coal and machinery, whereas twenty years later the figures were reversed, and a ship of 3,000 tons could carry 2,200 tons of cargo.
(21)   Maginnis, A. J.: "The Atlantic Ferry," 124.
(22)   Claxton, C.: "Log of the First Voyage of the Great Western."

In a lecture before the Section of the British Association on Mechanical Arts in September, 1836, he said:

"That, in the present state of the steam-engine, as applied to nautical purposes, he regarded a permanent and profitable communication between Great Britain and New York by steam vessels, making the voyage in one trip, as in a high degree improbable; that since the length of the voyage exceeds the present limits of steam power, it would be advisable to resolve it into the shortest practicable stages; and that, therefore, the most eligible point of departure would be the most western shores of the British Isles, and the first point of arrival the most eastern available parts of the western continent; and that, under such circumstances, the length of the trip, though it would come fully up to the present limit of this application of steam power, would, nevertheless, not exceed it; and that we might reasonably look for such a degree of improvement in the efficiency of marine engines as would render such an enterprise permanent and profitable."

Inasmuch as this speech was made nearly a year after Smith had founded his London company, it provoked a stirring discussion. The Valentia project, to Smith, was impracticable, because Valentia was not a large shipping port. "It is as easy to go to the moon as to go direct from a port in England to New York," Dr. Lardner was quoted as saying.[23] Smith and his followers sought to discredit the doctor by pointing out that his figures as to the longest voyages made by steamers were based upon voyages made prior to 1834 and that since 1834 considerable improvement had been made. In reply Dr. Lardner gave records of steamers subsequent to 1834, showing that a steamer could not carry coal enough to make the 3,200 mile voyage from Liverpool to New York.[24] He based his argument on the performances of a line of Admiralty steamers plying from Falmouth to Mediterranean ports, verified by the performances of other ocean-going craft, which demonstrated that two and four-tenths

---

(23) Liverpool "Albion" report of the speech before the British Association.
(24) "Edinburgh Review," Vol. 65 (April, 1837) pps. 69, 73, 74. "The long article in the 'Edinburgh Review' is from Dr. Lardner, a perfect quack and embarked in the Old Valentia Steamship Company, now defunct for twelve years . . . . . . The article in the 'Review' was begun, continued and ended with a view of opposing the British and American Steam Company." Junius to Henry Smith, July 15, 1837.

tons per horsepower was the total charge of fuel necessary to be supplied to a transatlantic steamer. Since a steamer of 1,200 tons, which would be 400 tons larger than the largest steamer whose records he had examined, if supplied with engine of 300 horsepower and fitted to carry sixty first-class passengers, would have capacity for only 450 tons of coal, it could go, according to his estimate, only 2,200 miles, which would be only two-thirds of the distance from Liverpool to New York.

"Whatever difference of opinion may exist as to the practicability of an Atlantic steam voyage," said the New York Journal of Commerce, in June, 1837, "it must be admitted upon all hands that its extent for an uninterrupted run comes to the extreme verge of the possible powers of steam navigation . . . . To be successful, the nearest points of approach to the Eastern and Western continents should be chosen as the points of arrival and departure, to increase the probabilities of success." It is a curious comment on the prevailing public opinion that Ithiel Town, the architect, who wrote an interesting prophecy of Atlantic steamships which appeared in the American Railroad Journal, November 24, 1832, did not acknowledge the authorship until 1838 when Smith's project had won success.

Business men were not sinking their money in what they considered impracticable experiments. The steam engine was changing the habits of men only slowly. Birmingham, where the steam engine was introduced in 1780, had 42 of them in 1815, and only 120 of them in 1830.[25] The textile factories of England, in 1835, employed only 50,000 mechanical horsepower, and of this one-fourth was obtained from water wheels. The power of steam did not work its great changes until 1850. Although steam transportation along the coasts and rivers had won a wider success than steam in any other form of activity, Junius Smith was a daring adventurer when he attempted to establish a line of steamers across the ocean. The chief fight he had was not with the elements—that came later—but with the diffidence of capitalists who refused even to listen to his plans.

Dr. Lardner's pessimistic outlook was in a measure vindicated, although not as he had prophesied, by the subsequent his-

(25) Day, Clive: "History of Commerce," 359.

1340 TONS   S. S. *Great Western*   450 H. P.

From a print published in New York in 1838, formerly in the collection of Dr. Charles K. Stillman

Presented to the Marine Historical Association, Inc.,

by Mrs. Harriet G. Stillman

tory of steam upon the Atlantic. The great Collins line did not stand the strain; the Cunard line triumphed over almost insuperable difficulties. Mechanics, in the early days of ocean liners, had to work day and night while the ship was in port repairing the damage done to the boilers and engines in their fight against the sea. How the loss of power caused by the paddles revolving in air has been done away with by the adoption of the screw, how escaping steam has been saved by the introduction of the compound engine, how iron and steel have been adapted to ship construction, giving opportunity for the building of larger ships, how the refinements of the engine have caused less weight and yet wonderfully increased the horsepower, how the quality of the coal from the mines has been improved, all these and many more problems were solved only after a generation of costly experiments.[26]

Yet Smith made up in zeal what he lacked in knowledge, and the fiercer the criticism and scorn of the so-called men of science, the more earnestly did he strive to convince the world that they were wrong.

As we have noted, Smith spoke of his proposed steam line to New York merchants in 1832. They said: "Go back to London, and if you form a company there, and succeed in the enterprise, we will come and join you." As a matter of fact, the help from America never materialized, owing to the commercial crisis of 1837,[27] but Smith hastened back to London. After a rapid passage of sixteen days into soundings, sixteen more days were frittered away in calm before he could make Plymouth.

In January 1833, he wrote to his nephew, Henry Smith, that he was ascertaining what steam ships were in port. "The transfer of the line of packets from Scanley's hands to Noah Schoville, Jr., and from the London to the St. Katherine's Docks will give great force to our active opposition to that concern," he said. "Indeed if I can succeed in establishing a line of steamers, they may hang their harps upon the willows as soon as they

---

(26)   Fry, H.: "History of North Atlantic Steam Navigation," divides the history into six periods: sail to wooden paddles, for speed; wood to iron hulls, for strength; paddle to screw, for economy; simple to compound engines, to save fuel; iron to steel hulls, for cost; single to twin screws, for safety.
(27)   A petition was presented to the New York legislature for an act of incorporation under the title American Steam Navigation Company, with a capital of $500,000, with the privilege of doubling it. "Atlantic Steam Ships"—Wiley & Putnam, 1838.

please. Thirty-two days from New York to Plymouth and forty to London is no trifle. Any ordinary sea-going steamer would have made it, the weather we had, in fifteen days with ease. I will not relinquish the project unless I find it absolutely impracticable."

He tried to interest the London and Edinburgh Steam Packet Company but was unsuccessful. He tried to get the *London Merchant,* as she could carry twenty days' supply of coals, and he thought that she was the only steam vessel in London suited to so long a voyage, but she was owned in shares, and he found no disposition "in this mass of clumsy headed fellows" to forward his views.

With the coming out of the prospectus in the spring of 1835,[28] he was hard at work to form a company with a capital of 100,000 pounds, in shares of 500 pounds each, to build two steamships, each of 1,000 tons and 300 horsepower, capable of carrying 450 tons of coal, with the expectation that two similar ships would be built in New York, to form a line of four steamers.

"You will remark," he wrote to his nephew, "that I have everything to do myself. I have to hunt up directors, appoint a banker, solicitor, auditors, etc. This takes much time. Gentlemen of London in good standing, whatever may be their occupation, have generally such a mass of business upon their hands that it is no easy matter to find those of the right stamp willing to take upon themselves the duties of a director. This increases my labor tenfold. For when I call upon a gentleman to offer him the office of director I must have a long talk and probably have to call two or three times before I get a final answer. If he declines why then I have to start again and go over the same ground with some other person. All this keeps me in a sweat in the month of July. The patience and labor of forming a company in London is beyond all that you can imagine. It is the worst place in the whole world to bring out a new thing, the best when it is done. One hundred thousand pounds is but a drop to the great moneyed interest of London. The difficulty is to overcome the affinity which that drop has for its old berth and to induce it to flow into a new channel. Do that, and it comes in a

---

(28)   See Appendix.

flood. All the old sailing interest of course is against me, because their craft is in danger."

With a "big name" on his board of directors, Smith felt that success was assured. The difficulty was to get that name. The Duke of Wellington sent a note to him on which was written: "The Duke has no leisure to receive the visits of gentlemen who have schemes for the alteration of the public establishments."[29] Which, probably, was no more encouraging than Smith had expected, but his aim was high. Sir John Read, of Read, Irving & Co., the leading bankers in London, who was a director of the Bank of England and a member of Parliament, assured Smith of his support by taking shares but he refused to have his name used as a director.

His list of temporary directors was not as excellent as he wished, but they were men of good standing. One was chairman of the Great Birmingham and London Railway Company, another was a retired East India House man, and others were a Portsmouth banker, a director of the General Steam Navigation Company, a Yankee shipper, a retired sugar merchant, and a "son of Isaac." He was having such good success that he decided to increase the capital stock to 500,000 pounds, add a few more directors, and "make an appeal to the public purse." Up to this time he had been devoting his time entirely to men of influence and had avoided publicity.

October 31, 1835, he wrote to his nephew,—"It was not my intention to come out with the steam company until next week. But finding my delay likely to be taken advantage of by others who begin to see the thing more clearly and think it too good a thing to be suffered to pass by them, I made a push yesterday, and am before the public today."

The public responded well to the call of the new prospectus and the British and American Steam Navigation Company, as it was now called, was organized within a few weeks. In nine days 6,000 shares at 100 pounds par had been applied for. The object of the investors was to get a greater dividend than the public funds gave. Many were women. Some were mere speculators. Merchants connected with the American trade did not respond.

---

(29)   Hunt's "Merchants Magazine," February, 1847.

November 19th the long hoped for "big name" was landed. Henry Bainbridge of Paget & Bainbridge, bankers, agreed to be a director, and with him came Charles Enderby, of almost equally high standing.

The work of Junius Smith, the promoter, was accomplished. The company was no longer a one man affair carried around on paper in Smith's pocket, but a group of highly influential moneyed men. At the meeting of the directors, November 25th, the two London bankers were in the saddle. More men were anxious to be directors than there were places. Bigger ships and bigger engines were talked of.

The "push," as Smith termed the bid for subscriptions, not only set the British and American Steam Navigation Company before the public but was the means of bringing its rival, the Great Western Steamship Company, into being. At a meeting of the directors of the Great Western Railway in October, 1835, one of the party spoke of the enormous length, as it then appeared, of the proposed railway from London to Bristol. Isambard K. Brunel, the famous engineer, exclaimed, "Why not make it longer, and have a steamboat to go from Bristol to New York, and call it the *Great Western*?" The suggestion was treated as a joke, but Mr. Brunel was serious and he talked with Christopher Claxton. "The appearance of the prospectus of the British and American Company," writes Mr. Claxton,[30] "brought matters to a point, and in November, 1835, a party of gentlemen connected with the railway, after a good deal of discussion, put down their names as ready to take shares in the event of due encouragement being given in Bristol." The company was not established by deed of settlement, however, until June of the following year.

Stirred, it is presumed, by the activity of the Bristol people, shippers in Liverpool sought to join Smith's company. In the spring of 1836, a delegation of Liverpool men came to London and conferred with the British and American directors. The result was an enlargement of the London company in 1836 in order to give the Liverpool people an interest. The idea was to establish a line of steamships from Liverpool to New York, as well

---

(30) "Log of the First Voyage of the Great Western."

as from London, to touch at Cork going and coming. It was proposed to augment the capital to one million, in 10,000 shares of 100 pounds each, instead of 500,000 pounds. The board of directors would sit in London only. "If successful," wrote Smith, "we shall ultimately combine the great commercial interests of Great Britain in one grand transatlantic steam navigation company, which will be sufficiently powerful and sufficiently extended to ward off all opposition."

The new directors were Joseph Robinson Pim of Liverpool, who was connected with the St. George & Dublin Steam Company, James Beale of Cork, and Paul Twigg of Dublin. The London directors, besides Bainbridge and Enderby, were Captain Thomas Larkins, Captain Robert Locke, Captain Robert Isacke, Colonel Aspinwall, the American Consul, and Junius Smith. The first ship was to run from London and the next from Liverpool. Messrs. Paget, Bainbridge & Co. were the bankers, Macgregor Laird the secretary and Junius Smith was to be the London shipping agent. When the Liverpool ship was in commission, the Pim interests were to have charge of her shipping arrangements. Macgregor Laird was probably recommended by the Liverpool interests. He had recently returned from an expedition up the river Niger in Africa in an iron steamship and had combated in public print the conservative views of Dr. Lardner.

The contract for the *British Queen*—at first named the *Royal Victoria*, in honor of the new queen just ascending the throne—was let in October to Curling and Young. She was to be the most splendid steamship ever built, designed especially for the New York and London trade, of 1,700 tons, measuring 235 feet between perpendiculars, 220 feet keel, 40 feet beam, with two engines of 225 horsepower each, 76 inch cylinders, and 9 foot stroke. She would carry 500 passengers, make the passage in fifteen days, and it was expected that she would be ready in March. The specifications subsequently were enlarged and Maginnis says that she was 275 feet long, 37½ feet broad and of 1863 tons, and had 700 horsepower engines.

While the *British Queen* was building, Junius Smith was writing to the newspapers. "You must keep printing," he wrote to his nephew later. "The editors themselves will not probably take the trouble to write, but are generally very glad of new matter upon a new subject. Therefore keep up a regular indirect fire, and be careful that nobody sees you, lest you get shot yourself. You must make up your mind to go to some expense out of your pocket. I have done so and have paid every shilling's expense for printing, etc. I dare say 100 pounds, and 150 pounds for advertising alone. You must keep the thing up, and insert paragraph after paragraph, one upon application for a charter, another on its being brought forward, upon its discussion, etc. Bennett says that in the United States the editors make all the great men. With regard to Bennett I think you are all wrong. You have nothing whatever to do with the man or his politics or his religion. If he were a very jackass and walked about the streets with your advertisement upon his rump, it would be just what you want. The object of advertising is to give publicity. You must not quarrel with any one, especially an editor."

Meanwhile the merry race between the pioneer steamship companies was on. Isambard K. Brunel, builder of the *Great Eastern* in later years, was the leading spirit in the Great Western Company. Macgregor Laird, a canny Scot, was pushing forward the construction of the *British Queen*. It was a question of who would get his vessel on the ocean first.

Suddenly the Glasgow firm, Claude Girdwood & Co., which was making the *British Queen's* engines went into bankruptcy. The work on the *Queen* came to a stop. The rival company was pushing ahead with renewed confidence, and the dreams of Junius Smith and Macgregor Laird seemed but mockery. The financial crisis in America had broken up Wadsworth & Smith, so that Henry Smith was deprived of the financial aid of his partner; London houses were falling with a crash; but all this was unheeded by Laird and Smith in their anxiety to win the applause of two continents.

It was the new little steamer *Sirius*, which was to run between Cork and Dublin, chartered for the occasion by Smith's company from the St. George Steam Packet Company, 178 feet long and of 703 tons register, that saved the day. While the *Great Western* was delayed by an accident, the *Sirius* slipped away, and after touching at Cork and experiencing a mutiny of the crew who were fearful, arrived in New York, April 22, 1838,

2016 TONS

S. S. British Queen

From a print in the Stokes Collection published in 1839
Reproduced by permission of the New York Public Library

500 H. P.

and was anchored at the Battery the next morning, before the *Great Western* arrived.

New York went wild. "The *Sirius*! The *Sirius*! The *Sirius*!" exclaimed the New York Weekly Herald. "Nothing is talked of in New York but about the *Sirius*. She is the first steam vessel that has arrived here from England."

"The *Sirius*[31] sailed from Cork on the evening of the 4th instant," said the New York Express of April 24, "and made the Highlands of New York at 6 o'clock P. M. on the 22d, making the passage in eighteen days. About 1 o'clock it was announced by telegraph that the steamer *Great Western* was off the Hook, when thousands poured down Broadway; and the Battery at 2 P. M. presented a brilliant appearance. The smoke of the *Great Western* was seen in the horizon ascending in black volumes long before her hull was visible. She approached the Battery through a fleet of rowboats and small craft, cheered by everyone. She soon ranged alongside the Castle, sailed around the *Sirius,* which saluted her, and the crowd from the wharves, Castle, boats, etc., gave three hearty cheers."

"The *Great Western* left Bristol April 7, and she was, April 23, only sixteen days, in New York, thus bringing England nearer to us than many parts of our own country. This has been done in a season of the year, not of summer sunshine, but of gales, storms, sleet, and hail—and steam navigation across the Atlantic is no longer an experiment, but a plain matter of fact."

"The arrival of two steamships from Europe," said the New York Journal of Commerce, "in such a way as to remove all doubt about the entire feasibility of navigating the Atlantic in that manner was a most important and gratifying result. It brings us within ten to fifteen days of Europe and gives us such increased certainty, as well as quickness, that a new era opens upon us."

"The *Great Western* came up in fine style. Her voyage has been almost in a straight line across the Atlantic. She took in 600 tons of coal, of which perhaps 200 remain. It is known to many of our readers that the steam apparatus of the *Sirius* is constructed on a new plan, by which all danger of explosion is avoided.

---

(31)   The "Sirius" was consigned to Wadsworth & Smith, Agents, 4 Jones Lane, New York.

Her boilers were supplied the whole way with fresh water, by means of a distilling apparatus, which converted salt water into fresh. The experiment with this ship (as well as the other) has been completely successful. Her passage was a rough one. Her steam was kept up and her headway without a moment's interruption. Her stock of 400 tons of coal is nearly exhausted. The passage of the *Sirius* was made in eighteen days from Cork; that of the *Great Western* in fifteen days from Bristol. The former is 700 tons burthen; the latter, 1,340."

The British consul congratulated the captain of the *Sirius*, a committee of aldermen visited both ships. Daniel Webster spoke at a banquet on the *Great Western*. "It is our fortune," said Mr. Webster, "to live at a new epoch. We behold two continents approaching each other. The skill of your countrymen, sir, and my countrymen, is annihilating space."

James Gordon Bennett, seeing the opportunity presented by a quick and reliable means of communication with the old world, sold out his library and furniture at auction in order to get ready cash, boarded the *Sirius* for her homeward journey, and hastened to the Continent to establish the news sources which made the New York Herald famous.[32]

As the *Sirius* neared the British coast she stopped to take the mail from the ten-gun brig *Tyrian* of Halifax which was rolling about in a dead calm. The incident made such an impression upon Joseph Howe, the Nova Scotia statesman, and his companions, that they labored to get a steamship mail line to Halifax.[33] Lord Glenelg sent word to Howe that he was deeply impressed with the importance of the subject and hoped an arrangement might be effected at an early period. The next month bids were advertised by the government, and Cunard secured the contract. "All honor," says Joseph Andrew Chisholm's Speeches and Public Letters of Joseph Howe "to the Nova Scotian who carried forward this great work with such signal success. But those gentlemen ought not to be forgotten who, at this early period, first turned the attention of British statesmen to a subject of so much importance." Nor should it be forgotten that the inspiration of

(32) "Memoirs of James Gordon Bennett."
(33) Fry, H.: "History of North Atlantic Steam Navigation," 58.

these men had its inception in the voyage of the *Sirius,* with which Smith's company had spiked the guns of Dr. Lardner.

If Junius Smith's claim to fame depended on the voyage of the steamship *Sirius* it would not be worth more than casual mention. The voyage really signified little, however vociferously the public cheered, and no one knew this better than Smith. By good luck with Hall's patent condensers, which saved the boilers from incrustations of salt, the little coasting steamer had made a rapid voyage from Cork to New York and just in the nick of time to take away the glory from the *Great Western.* But in principle the voyage differed little from those dare-devil dashes of the *Royal William* and other pioneer vessels, whose steam attracted publicity. There was no certainty that the *Sirius* would be able to continue her record, and it was not intended that she should. She was run at a loss. The real palm lay in the hands of the *Great Western,* a steamship built for the transatlantic trade and prepared to make regular trips across the ocean from port to port in fifteen days. It is significant, that notwithstanding the huzzas with which the voyage of the *Sirius* was greeted, the letters of Smith to his New York nephew have little to say concerning her. What Smith impatiently waited for was the maiden voyage of his big liner, the *British Queen.* It was business that he was looking for, rather than glory. Right here is the key to the claim that Smith has to fame, in comparison, for instance with the claims of the owners of the *Savannah* or the *Royal William.* The latter made use of the publicity connected with the voyages to sell their vessels. They may have had higher motives. But whether they did or not, their efforts ceased with the termination of their voyages. The efforts of Smith were bent toward a permanent system of transportation across the Atlantic by steam. His ship's hold could not be loaded with coal entirely, as in the case of the *Royal William.* There must be room for freight. He was not relying on a chance voyage of fifteen days. Every voyage must be one of fifteen days. The great mill pond must be as

---

The "Sirius" after her two transatlantic voyages, ran as a coasting steamer and was wrecked in 1847. Her commander, Lieutenant Roberts, remained with Smith's company and went down with the "President" in 1840. "The Great Western" made seventy-four transatlantic passages and was sold to the West India Royal Mail Steam Packet Company in 1847. She was broken up in 1857. A third pioneer company, the Trans-Atlantic Steam Ship Company, formed at Liverpool in 1838, put on two steamers to New York, the "Royal William" and the "Liverpool." Both were withdrawn in 1839.

well under control as the Mediterranean or the Hudson River.

His day of triumph came in the summer of 1839 when he and Laird accompanied the *British Queen* on her voyage to New York and the directors of the company gave them a banquet on their return. Laird, "after a few corduroy remarks," proposed "The Citizens of New York," and Junius Smith replied to the toast. The former Connecticut lawyer swelled a little beyond his usual size and brought forth applause which made the *Queen* tremble. "It was the first time these gentlemen had given me an opportunity to show off in this way," he wrote to his nephew, "and I put forth all my little powers." He was invited to be a director and agent of a steamship company to do business between London and Goole. With the *British Queen* running from London, and the *President* about to run from Liverpool, he thought that Bristol would dwindle and that the British and American Company would be in control of the shipping situation. Professor Benjamin Silliman of Yale College invited him to write for The American Journal of Sciences and Arts. He accepted the invitation and the letters were widely copied. They gave much information concerning steamships and recommendations for the future, and dealt at considerable length on the advantages of steamships in time of war. Professor Silliman inquired "What will a sailless ship do in mid-ocean when her machinery gives away?" and "How are the great warlike steam navies to be supplied with fuel?" and the London merchant came back with vigorous answers.

He was jealous of his claim as father of transatlantic steamship navigation, which the world regarded as the greatest triumph of the age. In this he was opposed by Laird. The Great Western people pointed with pride to the fact that their ship, the *Great Western*, was the first steam liner to actually engage in transatlantic business.[34] To the claim of Laird, Smith retorted that Laird was still in Africa when he was working to form the company, and to the claim of the Great Western people, he replied that it was not until the "push" of October 30, 1835, when he came before the public with his list of directors that the Great Western people began to consider the matter seriously. He asked

---

(34) Claxton, C.: Log of the First Voyage of the "Great Western," 1838. "Atlantic Steam-Ships," New York, 1838, gives a version more favorable to Smith.

his nephew in New York to see that a good history of the beginnings of the company was written, and he hoped that Washington Irving could be prevailed upon to write it. He aspired to knighthood, and the dream of attaining it was constantly before him. "See Silliman," he wrote his nephew, "if you can, before the *President* arrives, and tell him that Collegiate honors are of no use to me, but they hold out encouragement to others to embark in undertakings of great national importance, and generally speaking it is just all they may expect to receive for their labors. They ought to be rewarded by at least that which costs nothing. Cousin David as a member of the Corporation of Yale College might lend a hand, but I shall not say anything to him on the subject. It would come better from you. As soon as I am easy here in pecuniary matters so that my mind is unharassed, I shall endeavor to place matters right here."

The degree of Doctor of Laws was forthcoming at the Yale commencement of 1840. "We present to you this expression of our regard," wrote President Jeremiah Day, "not with the expectation of elevating the rank which you hold in public estimation but as a tribute of respect on account of the important service which you have rendered to Great Britain and your native land, especially by the enterprising projection, execution and completion of that novel method of navigating the Atlantic which brings the two countries in such eventful proximity to each other." The successful ship promoter was grateful for the honor. "A specific steam stamp not easily obliterated," he called it. "As soon as I have the means, for in this country titles of distinction are expensive patents, I intend to put in my claims. If I fail, my position will not be prejudiced. I shall only be plain Doctor."

While her father was wrapped up in his dreams of knighthood, Lucinda was having her dreams. "I am going to lose my daughter, out and out," he wrote to his nephew. "A young clergyman of the Church of England (Rev. Edward K. Maddock) threw a gold chain about her neck in Yorkshire, and she is captured. The young chap is now at my house red hot and ought to be seated upon a marble slab to cool him. I can't help it and must submit whether I will or not and so put as good a face upon the affair as I can. It is a most ungentlemanly thing to plunder me of my only child. There I shall be at Sydenham with a new house just furnished, all comfortable in absolute solitude. Nothing left but my great dog Prince, Jersey, and cat and two dozen fowls. Pshaw!"

The steamship business was as unkind as his daughter. The competition of the two lines and the packets was increased by the putting on of the subsidized Cunard steamer *Britannia*. He had thirty shares in his company that paid him nothing and he could not get back the money he had expended. John Smith, a grandnephew in England, owed him 600 pounds. The crash came with the wreck of the *President*. This meant the end of the company, the sale of the *British Queen* to the Belgian government, and the ruin of Smith's career. The Great Western company also lost a vessel and the Cunard company was left alone on the seas.

The fate of the *President* was never known. She was lost in a gale off George's Bank, after she had steamed from New York for Liverpool, March 11, 1841, in command of Captain Roberts. Some said she "broke her back" because of her great length for a wooden ship. Others said she ran into an iceberg. She carried 110 souls, some of whom were distinguished passengers. An official investigation revealed no negligence on the part of the company.[35]

"What sighs have been wafted after that ship!" wrote Washington Irving of the *President*. "What prayers offered up at the deserted fireside of home! How often has the sister, the mother, pored over the daily news to catch some casual intelligence of this rover of the deep! How has expectation darkened into anxiety—anxiety into dread—and dread into despair! Alas! not one memento shall ever return for love to cherish. All that shall ever be known is—that she sailed from her port—and was never heard of more."[36]

Had she returned to shore, Washington Irving might have written that history of steam navigation, and Junius Smith might have been a knight instead of Cunard and the Crystal Palace might never have marred that beautiful estate at Sydenham. But with the wreck of the *President,* the wings of Junius Smith were clipped. His business was gone; his daughter was in India with

---

(35) Lazelle, W.: "Steamboat Disasters."
(36) Lazelle, W.: "Steamboat Disasters."

2366 TONS

S. S. *President*

From a print in the Stokes Collection published in 1840
Reproduced by permission of the New York Public Library

600 H. P.

her chaplain husband;[37] there was no tie to keep him in England, and he returned in the autumn of 1843 to the democratic land of his birth—merely a doctor.

Back in America after an absence of 38 years, at the home of his nephew Henry Smith in Astoria, L. I., he worked diligently in the garden, making it blossom with all the bloom and regularity of an English country estate. He wrote twenty letters in answer to Dickens's American Notes, and sought to have them published under the name of Timothy Tickler. Two of them were on slavery, suggesting means of abolition. He wrote articles for Hunt's Merchants Magazine on such subjects as "The Warehousing System" and "Production and Export of Breadstuffs."

Then he took up his old love, steam navigation, seeking to interest American capitalists. He delivered a stirring address before the American Institute in New York in 1844. The success of Cunard was his inspiration. If he could start a line from New York to England with a subsidy from the United States government, he would win back his laurels. Inasmuch as the Secretary of the Navy and the heads of other departments said that they were powerless to grant a subsidy, he went to Washington and sought to obtain the necessary empowering act from Congress. The bill which he fathered gave the Postmaster-General power to contract with American citizens for American vessels to carry the mails for a period greater than four years but not greater than ten years. The ships were to be used by the government in war time. Preference was to be given to the bidder who would carry the mail in steamships.

President Tyler gave the project a good send-off by urging a steam mail line in his message of December 3, 1844. The bill was introduced in the Senate by Senator William D. Merrick of Maryland, who secured its passage. When it came into the House, February 15, Congressman Joseph Grinnell of Massachusetts championed it and it was passed in the exciting turmoil of March 3, the eve of President Tyler's retirement, a few minutes

---

(37) His daughter, Mrs. Edward K. Maddock, had four children but their grandfather saw none of them. The oldest boy died in India. The others were: Henry Edward Maddock, born December 31, 1844, who became Dean of York; Junius Arthur, born December 3, 1848, some of whose children settled in California, and Emily Mary, born March 24, 1852, who married De John Pritchard and was still living January 1, 1912, in Wales. Her one son, John, was then in Trinity College, Cambridge.

before midnight, after a repeated demand for its consideration by Congressman John Pendleton Kennedy of Maryland.[38]

Junius Smith was again triumphant. He expected to obtain the contract for carrying the mails from this country to England. But fate was against him in the person of Cave Johnson, the new Postmaster-General appointed by President Polk, who gave the contract to a line to be run by Bremen. As Smith predicted, the Bremen line did not succeed, but this did Smith no good, and he dropped his steamship plans in disgust. He had been underbid by rival interests, as the Great Western company had been beaten out by Cunard.

It was E. K. Collins who reaped the reward. Collins came forth with a proposal to establish a line to Liverpool, took the matter over the Postmaster-General's head, and got Congress to authorize the line. The special act which he obtained was passed "in pursuance of the law of March 3, 1845." This was the law prepared by Smith.

In December, 1848, Smith went to Greenville, S. C., where he experimented in raising tea on his 200-acre farm. His enthusiasm for tea cultivation in the United States was as great as that for transatlantic steamship navigation but he did not live long to enjoy his new hobby. He was assaulted by ruffians while alone in his house just before Christmas, 1851, and died January 22, 1853, aged 72.

Tea farming has not been profitable in the United States owing to competition from the Orient with its cheap labor. But if the tea venture has not turned out as Smith would have wished, the success of his main life work, the promotion of steam navigation upon the ocean, has exceeded all his expectations.

His failure to see obstacles, a characteristic which in later years caused the ruin of steamship managers, made him an ideal promoter, a tower of strength before the timid investor, whose every objection was answered by a strong personality with a confidence unshaken and an eloquence that was invincible. The experiments of the engineers would not have been made but for the voyages of the liners. The liners would not have ventured unless some company sent them. And no company would have existed

---

(38) "Congressional Globe," Second Session Twenty-eighth Congress, pp. 395-396.

had not some idealist inveigled the cold cash from the pockets of the investors. Smith had the talent to lead men into projects whose only object would have been the lining of his own pockets. It is to his credit that his aim was nobler than this and that he himself became a poor man in the prosecution of his venture. Without his peculiar service, the beginnings of Atlantic steam navigation would have been delayed for years. London, as Smith pointed out, was the worst place in the world to bring out a new thing, the best when it is done. The difficulty was to overcome the affinity which the first drop of money had for its berth and to induce it to flow into a new channel. From the day that the unaided efforts of Junius Smith tapped the rock and started the first few drops to flowing, a steady stream of money has poured forth from Great Britain into the Atlantic ocean, and because of her later liberality she has won and maintained supremacy of the seas.

The First Prospectus

June, 1835

Union Line of Steam Packet Ships
From London to New York

No part of the world presents so great an opening for the successful employment of steam Ships as the Line from London to New York. The Continent of Europe, the Continent of America, and the British Dominions, make this route their common road. The single fact, that 50,000 individuals landed in New York in 1834, from this Country only, affords undeniable evidence that the scope for such an undertaking is sufficiently ample. By embarking at Portsmouth, whence it is proposed that the Ships shall take their final departure, the access to this Line from the Continent is easy; and the course by way of Liverpool will be in some measure superseded by the greater certainty and expeditions of Steam Navigation.

It is therefore proposed to form a Line, composed of Two British and Two American Steam Ships of 1,000 tons each, which will be sufficient to keep up a communication twice a month to and from New York. The reason for uniting the two classes of ships in one Line must be obvious to those acquainted with the trade; to those who are not, it may be proper to state, that British Ships, by Treaty of Commerce, are not permitted to take foreign and colonial goods to the United States; they must be shipped in American bottoms. On the other hand, American Ships are not permitted to bring colonial or foreign goods to England, except for exportation only. By the union of both, all descriptions of goods are secured.

Measures have already been taken to secure the building of Two Steamers in New York; but the interest, so far as regards the ships, will be separate and distinct, and combined only as comprising part of the same Line. Four steam ships will make as many passages in twelve months as eight sailing ships; and the investment will not equal the cost of eight sailing ships of equal tonnage.

The two ships intended to be built of 1,000 tons each, and 300 horse-power, with all their equipments complete, and ready for sea, are estimated to cost £35,000 each.

It is proposed to form a Company with a subscribed Capital of £100,000 in Shares of £500 each, to be called for in such sums and at such times, giving a month's notice, as the progress of the work may require.

The following is the result of minute calculations of practical gentlemen well acquainted with the trade:

	£	s.	d.
Annual expense of commanders, mates, engineers, firemen, seamen, oil, tallow and incidental expenses, ...	1,928	0	0
Rate to cover wear and tear, insurance, repairs, renewals, etc., may be taken at 20 per cent. upon prime cost, ...	7,000	0	0
Fuel for six voyages out and home, 4,000 tons, at 25 s., ...	5,000	0	0
Total annual expense of navigation for each ship, equal to £2,321 a voyage, ...	£13,928	0	0

A vessel of the size named will carry 450 tons of coal, or 20 days' supply, 150 tons dead weight, 400 tons measurement goods, 400 passengers, and one month's provisions, and will perform her passages from and to Portsmouth upon an average in 13 to 14 days.

Estimated Receipts upon One Passage out to New York:

150 tons dead weight, @ 25s,	£ 187	10				
400 tons measurement goods, @ 40s,	800	0	£ 987	10	0	
60 Cabin passengers, @ £30 each,	1,800	0				
80 Second cabin passengers @ £20 each,	1,600	0				
100 Steerage passengers, @ £10 each,	1,000	0		0	0	
240	4,400	0				
Less for children	550	0	3,850	0	0	
Total receipt,			£4,837	10	0	

This is supposing the ship has an average number of only 240 passengers, instead of her full complement of 400; because in the winter months it is not probable that she would be full. But it is fair to calculate, that these ships would take all the specie shipped to and from New York, which would make a large item in the freight, and is omitted in this estimate.

Expenses Independent of Those Incidental to the Floating Establishment:

Provisions for 30 days, cabin stores, outfit, etc.,	£ 600	0	0
Port Charges,	120	0	0
Commission of management, including brokerage, counting-house, expenses, clerks, etc., 5 per cent.,	240	0	0
	960	0	0
One month's floating expenses,	1,160	0	0
	£2,120	0	0
Gross receipts out,	£4,837	10	0
Gross expenses,	2,120	0	0
Monthly profit *out* for each ship,	£2,717	10	0

There is no reason to suppose that the receipts would be less on her return passage than on her outward. If the steerage passage-money be less, the freight would be double; because, being a British ship, she can bring valuable Foreign goods, which pay a larger freight than American goods. But suppose she makes a net freight and passage-money of £2,000 home, instead of £2,717, 10s., and it cannot upon any reasonable calculation be less, it will give a profit of £4,717, 10s. upon each voyage, allowing two months for its completion.

This plan is respectfully submitted by Mr. JUNIUS SMITH, Agent for the Union Line of Sailing Ships to New York, to those who may feel disposed to uphold the British interests connected with the United States, and who see the subject in the light that he does. He will take Four Shares in the Company: but as he is fully acquainted with the practical part of the business, and has a connexion and an interest formed, he thinks it fair and right that it should be understood that he is to act as Ship's Husband in loading and receiving the consignment of the Ships in London, and that his friends who have undertaken to establish the American part of the Line in New York should enjoy the same privilege there, upon the usual and customary commission of 5 per cent., including brokerage, clerk hire, and counting-house expenses.

As soon as the Shares are subscribed, a Meeting of the Proprietors will be called to nominate and appoint a Committee to superintend the making of contracts for building the Ships, to appoint an Auditor of Accounts, Banker, etc.

It is intended that the first Ship shall sail 1st April next, and the second the 1st May; and that the American Ships shall sail the 16th of each month.

It is not intended to give publicity to this proposal through the medium of the public journals, or to make it a stock-jobbing business in any way, but rather to recommend the subject as one calculated for a safe, permanent, and profitable investment.

The annexed undertaking will be sufficient until a private Meeting of the Subscribers is called.

G. Eccles, Printer, 101, Fenchurch Street.

The undersigned will take   Shares in the
LONDON AND NEW YORK UNION STEAM PACKET
NAVIGATION COMPANY, and hereby agrees to pay the
Instalments as specified in the Prospectus of the said Company.

To Mr. JUNIUS SMITH,
    New York Packet Office,
        4 Fen Court, Fenchurch Street.

    To be sent in on or before the 1st July.

(In Junius Smith's handwriting)

    The Liverpool Albion of the 6th Inst. has an article upon
the prospectus which I saw yesterday. As to coals you will perceive that from New York to England we stand upon precisely
same footing, and the only difference in expense will be the difference of the price of coals at Liverpool and at Portsmouth,
which cannot be anything material as we can get our coals delivered at Portsmouth for 15/ or 16/ ton. This for your answer
to all opponents.

    The thing makes much talk here and is highly approved.

9th July, 1835.   J. S.

    (On the back of this prospectus is the endorsement by
Henry Smith: Prospectus of Steam Ships. 1st Prospectus, June,
1835.)

THE SECOND PROSPECTUS
Oct. 31, 1835

    Although much appears in Junius's letters to his nephew
Henry about the second prospectus and two copies were enclosed
for Henry's use no copy can be found among the correspondence.
David B. Tyler in his "Steam Conquers the Atlantic" mentions a
copy of this prospectus in the British Museum. The second prospectus differs from the first in that it was intended for public
perusal and first bears the name British & American Steam Navigation Co.

APPENDIX II

Typical Contemporary Newspaper Comment

ARRIVAL OF FIRST STEAMSHIPS

New York Evening Post, April 24, 1838.

"THE STEAM PACKETS.—The arrival yesterday of the steam packets *Sirius* and *Great Western* caused in this city that stir of eager curiosity and speculation which every new enterprise of any magnitude awakens in this excitable community. The Battery was thronged yesterday morning with thousands of persons of both sexes, assembled to look on the *Sirius*, the vessel which had crossed the Atlantic by the power of steam, as she lay anchored near at hand, gracefully shaped, painted black all over, the water around her covered with boats filled with people passing and repassing, some conveying and some bringing back those who desired to go aboard. An American seventy-four in one of the ports of the Mediterranean, or of South America, would hardly be surrounded with a greater throng of the natives.

When the *Great Western*, at a later hour, was seen ploughing her way through the waters toward the city, a prodigious mass, blacker if possible than her predecessor, the crowd became more numerous, and the whole bay, to a great distance, was dotted with boats, as if everything that could be moved by oars had left its place at the wharves. It seemed, in fact, a kind of triumphal entry.

The problem of the practicability of establishing a regular intercourse by steam between Europe and America is considered to be solved by the arrival of these vessels, notwithstanding the calculations of certain ingenious men in England, at the head of whom is Dr. Lardner, who have proved by figures that the thing is impossible."

APPRAISAL OF JUNIUS SMITH'S ACHIEVEMENT

Morning Journal, New York.
September 13, 1839.

"In 1832, when Junius Smith, Esq., a true Yankee, from the state of Connecticut, first proposed navigating the Atlantic with steam, he was laughed at, told to build a railroad to the moon first, and then run steam ships to New York. He persevered, however, and we have already witnessed the success of his splendid conception."

CPSIA information can be obtained
at www.ICGtesting.com
Printed in the USA
BVHW031456150719
553494BV00004B/31/P